A SHAKESPEARE-INSPIRED TALE

Romeo

ART DIRECTION & TEXT BY NICOLE MALONEY

PAINTINGS BY TREG MILLER

Juliet

PUBLISHED BY 2M MEDIA, LOS ANGELES
©2011 by Nicole Maloney

ISBN: 978-0-9836433-0-2

*For information regarding permission, email Nicole Maloney at nicole@nicolemaloney.com
or visit the websites http://www.nicolemaloney.com or http://www.tregmiller.com.*

Romeo Loves Juliet, A Shakespeare-inspired Tale is part of an entire series of Shakespeare stories and original paintings.
Other titles in print include: *Much Ado, A Shakespeare-Inspired Tale.*
Titles available in 2012 include: *Hamlet, Henry V, Midsummer Nights Dream* and *Macbeth.*

Printed in the U.S.A.

Designed by Elisa Leone
THE PAINTINGS IN THIS BOOK ARE ORIGINAL ACRYLICS ON WATERCOLOR PAPER

FOR

KIDS OF ALL AGES

PUT THE BOOK DOWN AND DO TEN JUMPING JACKS

CLEAN YOUR ROOM

STOP EVERYTHING AND READ, READ, READ

SHAKESPEARE ROCKS!

THIS TALE OF TRUE LOVE HAPPENED LONG, LONG AGO

ABOUT A GIRL NAMED JULIET AND A BOY NAMED ROMEO

IT IS SET IN THE SMALL TOWN OF VERONA, ITALY

WHERE THESE TWO FEUDING FAMILIES LIVED ACTUALLY

WHAT HAPPENED NEXT AS YOU CAN GUESS

BECAME A ROMANTIC TALE

CUPID SHOT ARROWS FROM HIS BOW

AND INTO THE HEART OF ROMEO,THE MALE

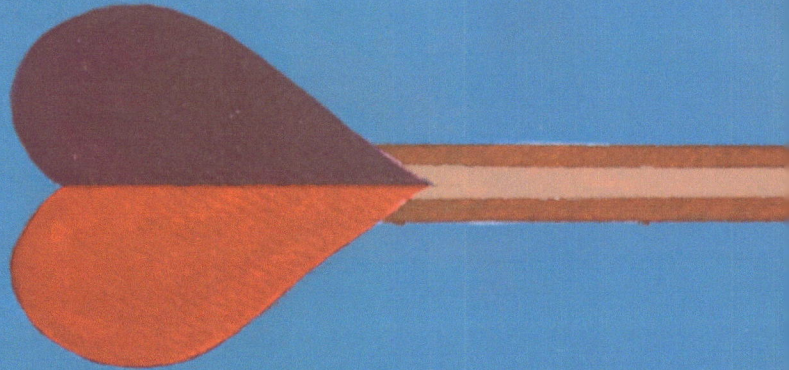

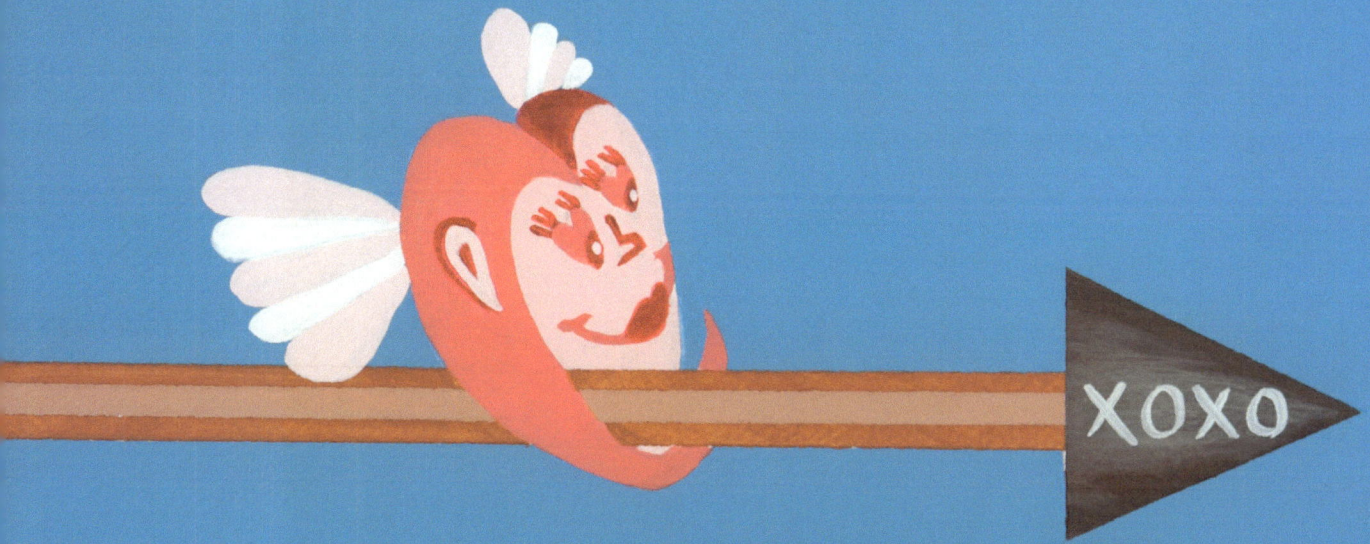

XOXO

IT WAS A MESS,
A FLOP-FLIP-FLOP
THEIR LOVE WAS TRUE,
A HOP-HIP-HOP

Hear Ye! Hear Ye!

Romeo loves Juliet

"ROMEO LOVES JULIET"

THE NEWS HAD SPREAD AROUND

WHEN **ROMEO** WALKED DOWN THE STREET

HIS FEET WERE **OFF THE GROUND**

EVERYWHERE THAT ROMEO WENT

THERE ALWAYS WAS A CROWD

THEY HAD TO LOOK WAY-WAY-WAY-WAY UP

HIS HEAD WAS IN THE

CLOUDS!

"JULIET LOVES ROMEO"

THAT'S WHAT THE FOLKS DID SAY

WHEN JULIET FELT ROMEO'S LOVE

HER HEART WAS HIS THAT DAY

EACH NEW DAY THEY FELL MORE

IN LOVE-LOVE-LOVE

THE TWO HAD LONGED TO WED

BUT A SECRET...THEY MUST KEEP

IT OR HER FAMOUS WORDS WOULD

NEVER HAVE BEEN SAID

"WHEREFORE ART THOU ROMEO?"

JULIET CALLED OUT ONE NIGHT

FROM BALCONY SHE GAZED BELOW

YET ROMEO WAS NOT IN SIGHT

IT WAS A MESS,
A FLOP-FLIP-FLOP
THEIR LOVE WAS TRUE.
A HOP-HIP-HOP

REMEMBER THAT GREAT BIG CLOUD

ABOVE THAT SWALLOWED ROMEO'S HEAD?

IF THE SKIES WERE CLEAR THAT DAY

HE MIGHT HAVE HEARD JULIET INSTEAD!

THEIR SECRET PLAN TO GO AWAY

DID NOT WORK OUT AS PLANNED

INSTEAD THEIR TIME TOGETHER WAS BRIEF

AND LASTED ONLY WHILE ON THIS LAND

THIS TALE OF TRUE LOVE

IS ONE TO REMEMBER

IT IS FAMOUS BY ITS MAKER

THERE IS NOTHING MORE POWERFUL THAN TRUE LOVE

FOR ROMEO WENT TO HEAVEN TO TAKE HER

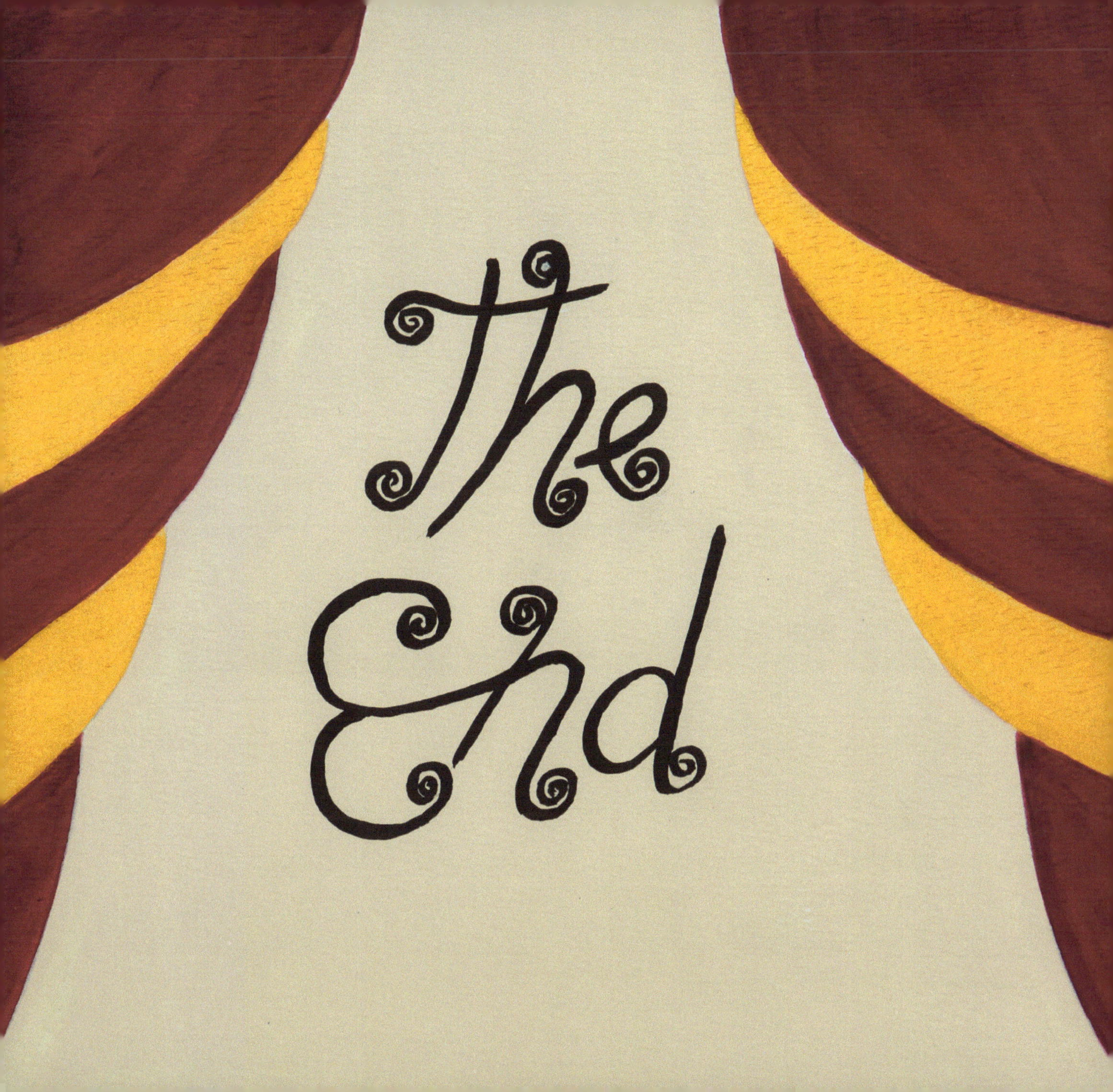
The End

ROMEO AND JULIET BY WILLIAM SHAKESPEARE

Romeo and Juliet is one of Shakespeare's most famous tragedies. The play is set in Verona, Italy. Two of the town's most significant families, the Montagues and the Capulets, have been engaged in a long and bitter feud and are sworn enemies. The Prince of Verona is so fed up with the public feuding between the Montague and Capulet supporters that he declares any future breach of peace will be punishable by death.

In the beginning, Romeo is infatuated with another girl. At the same time, Juliet's father has already been presented with an offer for his daughter's hand in marriage. Juliet is only thirteen. The chance these two will ever meet is slim.

Not so fast…young hearts love a grand party. Romeo goes to the ball hoping to find another girl, but instead, he sees Juliet for the first time. He feels as if his breath has been taken away when he looks into her eyes. They are desolate when they realize each other's true identities as a Montague and a Capulet, but their feelings of love and excitement for each other are undimmed. They proclaim their love for one another and decide to get married in secret the next day.

But boys will be boys. A fight ensues between Juliet's cousin, Tybalt, and Romeo's best friend, Mercutio. Romeo wants to fight only with words, but Tybalt and Mercutio don't agree. Romeo tries to intervene in the fight but it is too late. Tybalt kills Mercutio. Seeing his best friend stand up for him and then dying for him, Romeo attacks Tybalt and slays him.

Romeo realizes the consequences of his actions and hides. That night, Romeo joins Juliet in her chamber and they again pronounce their love for one another.

Unaware of Juliet's love for Romeo, her parents agree to offer her hand in marriage to another man. Juliet feels such deep pain that she announces she would rather die than marry another man. The Friar offers Juliet a magical potion that will make everyone believe she is dead. Juliet is told to drink it the night before the arranged marriage. The Friar promises to send word to Romeo of this plan.

Juliet drinks the magical potion. Everyone believes Juliet is dead so her body is laid in the Capulet crypt. Romeo hears of her death before the message from the Friar arrives. Romeo rushes to Juliet to see her once again. Romeo's heart is broken so he drinks poison. Juliet awakes only to find her true love, Romeo, dead at her side. Juliet cannot bear the grief and stabs herself with Romeo's dagger. They would rather be together in heaven than apart on earth.

The Montagues and Capulets discover the truth of their children's love for one another and how it led them to their deaths. They decide to reconcile their differences and put an end to their bitter and violent fighting.

In the end, the families did right, but it was too late to save Romeo and Juliet.

The story of *Romeo Loves Juliet* is inspired by Shakespeare's famous play, *Romeo and Juliet*

www.ingramcontent.com/pod-product-compliance
Lightning Source LLC
Chambersburg PA
CBHW041243040426

42445CB00004B/126